# LIKE HEADLINES
## New and Selected Poems

*Nancy Dillingham*

*Critical Praise for the Poetry of Nancy Dillingham*

"This is a fine, strong book, one for any poet to be proud of, and it shows [Dillingham's] excellences to grand advantage. . . . This is a terrific work, admirable and enviable."
**-Fred Chappell**, author of *A Shadow All of Light* and *Ancestors and Others*

"Nancy Dillingham writes of times past and time passing, and she does so with a beautiful balance of concision and eloquence."
**-Ron Rash**, author of *Waking* and *Something New and Strange*

"History, the land, and family beckon with a 'finely formed hand.' The reader will enjoy the journey and the shining details placed on their path."
**-Katherine Soniat**, author of *The Swing Girl*, and *A Raft, A Boat, A Bridge*

"Imagistic, narrative, dense as a laurel thicket, precise as a lightning strike, these poems catch at your spirit. As a master carver removes to reveal essence, this poet pares away verbiage. The result is stellar—poems blindingly immediate as sticking tongue to frozen metal. Dillingham's poems tap our emotional keyboard with deft and delicate yet meaty and strong vocabulary."
**-Celia Miles**, author of *Mattie's Girl: An Appalachian Childhood* and *Sarranda*

"Dillingham has developed a mastery of her craft as well as a distinctive style. The wondrous, grim, and familial come to light in compact lines that are both facets of and links in the narrative. What we get is poetic . . . and accessible."
**-Rob Neufeld**, author, historian, and book editor, *Asheville Citizen-Times*

"Dillingham's poems offer the sharp perception, clear imagery, and piercing irony found in Emily Dickinson's verse. In her concise poem 'The Bonnie Parker Monologue,' Dillingham captures the outlaw's

postmortem reflection: 'On that fateful May day/ambushed and betrayed/I lay vivid and dead/in my rusty red dress.' Equally chilling and compellingly intimate is the terse 'Sylvia Plath Ruminating.' Here we find Plath's perception of her suicide as 'warm and comforting here/in the oven.' In perhaps Dillingham's most haunting poem 'In the Garden,' a woman discovers a dead man 'Henry/[a]black-as-indigo/field hand' lying dead 'still/as some old/scarecrow,' a bird pecking out his eye 'as if his face were/a discarded corncob.' In her poems, Dillingham explores a world of historical figures, country folks, and modern lovers. But be forewarned: Dillingham pulls no punches to ensure her readers a deeply affecting experience."
-**Julia Nunnally Duncan**, author of *A Place That Was Home* and *A Part of Me*

"Death and life and a blissful, clever wordcrafting highlight this exquisite book of poetry. Nancy Dillingham sees the world through a lens that is bright and dark and relentless. . . . There is power here and ragged glory."
-**Byron Ballard**, folklorist, author, *Asfidity* and *Mad-Stories*

"Nancy Dillingham crafts poems that explore a complex landscape, both emotional and geographical. They reveal universal themes of love, loss, birth, [and] death."
-**Pat Riviere-Seel**, author of *The Serial Killer's Daughter* and *Nothing Below but Air*

"Reading Dillingham's work is like swimming in a jade pool where the surface water is brilliant and inviting—but underneath, where sunlight can't penetrate, a disturbing darkness lurks."
-**Bill Brooks**, author of *The Stone Garden: The Epic Life of Billy the Kid*

"Nancy Dillingham is a conscious stylist, well-read and ironic. I am in awe of her lilting lines, her use of rhymes, exact, fake (faux), and internal. I so love her poetry's unbrutalized honesty. Somehow her poetry captures the curves and sinews, the grist and grit of her mountain heritage."
-**Eston Roberts**, poet, novelist, philosopher

Cover art: "Mount Pisgah Moment," watercolor by Sandra Brugh Moore
Author Photo: Bill Mosher
Cover and Interior Design: Greg Gilpin, Graphic Art Center, Inc.

Red Dirt Press
1831 N. Park Ave.
Shawnee, OK 74804
www.reddirtpress.net

ISBN 978-1-7327383-1-7

## Also by Nancy Dillingham

**Poetry and Short Fiction**

*Tender Curiosities: Poems*
*More Frailer than Flowers: Poems*
*Horizons: Poems*
*1950: Poems*
*Americana Rural*
*Home: Poems*
*Colloquy in Black and White: Poems*
*Thanks for the Dark but That's Not Home: Poems and Stories*
*First Light: Poems*
*The Ambiguity of Morning*
*New Ground*

**Anthologies** (co-editor)

*Christmas Presence from 45 Western North Carolina Women
    Writers*
*Clothes Lines from 75 Western North Carolina Women Writers*
*Women's Spaces Women's Places from 50 Western North Carolina
    Women Writers*
*It's All Relative: Tales from the Tree from 50 Western North
    Carolina Women Writers*

**In Collaboration**

*Reflections in a River: Photographs by Joan Medlicott
    Haiku by Nancy Dillingham*

**Memoir** (fictional)

*Buried Lives: Memoir of a Survivor*

For Kay

*. . .light begins here . . .*
*Lets me be.*
*Here. Where I am.*

Kathryn Stripling Byer
1944-2017

# Contents

## Love Hurts

## Our House

## God Bless The Child

## If I Had A Bell

## Pet Sounds

## When The Deal Goes Down

*. . . the clouds are like headlines*
*upon a new front-page sky.*

Tom Waits

# Introduction
## Headlines, Heartlines
**❀❀❀**

Ezra Pound, that cranky ringmaster of twentieth-century American poetry, offered this definition: "Poetry is news that stays news." His point, that strong poetry is always important, fresh, and urgent, would be soberly received by many an earnest striver in the art, even those who had never heard of Pound. Some poets had always pushed onward to take the further step of distilling their news to forms that almost resemble headlines, composing slender verses to partially reveal, or to hint at, narratives of mysterious complexity. Sometimes the brief poems serve as "hook" headlines that make readers desirous to know more or to try to construct narratives into which such sharp revelations can fit.

Emily Dickinson, whom Nancy Dillingham alludes to in several of her pieces, furnishes us with numerous "headline" poems of bright impact:

Tell all the Truth but tell it slant—
Success in Circuit lies
Too bright for our infirm Delight
The Truth's superb surprise
As Lightning to the Children eased
With explanation kind
The Truth must dazzle gradually
Or every man be blind—

Ancient Chinese poets like Wang Wei, Han Yu, Li He and others specialized in condensing whole chronicles of joy, sadness, and loneliness into the minimum of lines. Here is Li Bai (701-762), "Brooding in the Still Night":

Bright moonlight before my bed.
At first I think the floor is all frost.
I gaze up at the mountain moon,
Then drop my head in a dream of home.

These two poets are very different from each other and Nancy Dillingham is different from both. But when I read the lines of Li Bai, Dillingham's "Dreamscape" advances readily to mind:

Swimming in silver
I rise
my life
a skin I have shed

Eyes glittering
graceful as a snake
I stir my starry skies
and breathe like Eve

onto my lover's bed

I count only thirty-one words needed to imply a tumultuous novel of love, passion, temptation, possible betrayal, fresh resolve, and fateful consequence. I feel certain that if these nine lines were fleshed out in prose to novel length, the dense five hundred pages would strike me with less impact.

It is by fine distillation that we gather our most powerful spirits.

Perhaps any poet's New and Selected volume may be read as distilled autobiography and in a large sense that is true of *Like Headlines*. Yet Dillingham has taken delightful pains to open out biography to include social, historical, and artistic concerns. Only the section titled "Our House" approaches autobiographical material in fairly straightforward manner. Other sections address the positions of women in society, the complexities of childhood, love and marriage, and social protest. The final section, "When the Deal Goes Down," reminds us wryly, tenderly, and sorrowfully that mortality is a temporary condition, as the faithful woman who comes to tend graves demonstrates with her annual ritual. "She will brush honeysuckle hair/from ancient faces/ pluck star grass from their eyes." ("Tending the Graves") Upon reading these lines I had to take three breaths to steady myself, startled to find in the imagery a vivid past, present, and future displayed in this act of solitary devotion.

It is a function of rituals such as grave-tending to convey a sense of hushed timelessness. Consider, for example, how the noisiness of a large family dinner is stilled as soon as one of the elders is called to say grace. The silence of a very small assembly can seem vast. Even the most casual incidents of our lives adopt the posture of ritual when we study them as images. In "Woman on the Porch" the seated figure is immersed in a private timelessness; she is in the present moment but not of it; the *apartness* she embodies makes her appear as much a hallowed icon as a human figure. A memory removes her from our time-frame so thoroughly that she is no longer conscious of it, "so far back//into the black void/she can no longer/hear the birds sing."

"Lighting the Fire" might almost be regarded as a companion piece to "Woman on the Porch." Again, a lone figure is removed from present time by force of memory. The sight of crushed flowers in a field brings back to her memories not only of youthful ardor but of the pains resulting from such passion. When she returns to her lonely cabin, she sets fire to those memories. Her driving passion now is to try to forget:

> Alone in her cabin
> she folds her memories
> in the lockbox of her brain
>
> strikes a match
> lights the fire
> watches it burn

The final stanza of three lines, each containing three words, sounds out a determined, stern resolution. She wills herself to forget. But the "lockbox" is metaphorical, as are the match and the cleansing fire. When next she opens the lockbox, she must strike another useless match. Barring their loss to dementia, the documents of grievous memory are impervious to destruction.

Now and again our poet seems to try on the good old Imagist mode, catching the essence of a moment with the eyes of an artful photographer, presenting a picture that hints of no past history or implies no future destiny. "Park Swing" is a poem that Pound as Imagist might envy:

> Little girls
> with horizontal hair

and umbrella dresses
punch holes in the sky

Here is a frozen instant that is no more than it is. —Wait now ... Little girls punching holes in the sky? Perhaps they will grow up to become Sister Rosetta Tharpe, Sylvia Plath, or Amelia Earhart. Their losses have made our sky emptier, and Dillingham has opened this collection with poems about them. Though offering an array of apparently different subjects, *Like Headlines* is unified in unobvious but powerful ways. There is probably no poem included that does not in some manner of extension touch upon most of the other poems.

A chosen moment never passes into oblivion, even if soundless, as when the father trims his young daughter's hair, in "Jole Blon":

Silences piling up
like shorn locks

on the floor
of the high front porch

"Silences piling up" is a phrase descriptive of many another Dillingham poem. We might compare "Temptation," "Old Age Penchant," "End Game," "Omen," "Shivaree," and further instances of often ominous portent in which we wait both for the future to happen and for the past to subside.

In fact, I think Silences Piling Up would make a good title for the next collection by Nancy Dillingham. I anticipate eagerly that signal event. You may picture me holding my breath. Meanwhile, here is *Like Headlines* to keep me harmonious company.

-**Fred Chappell**

# I Am Woman

**Maid of Orleans**
**1412-1431**


After they burned
Joan of Arc at the stake

the English raked
back the coals

to expose
her charred body

so no one could claim
she had escaped

then burned her remains
twice more

before casting them
into the Seine

**Anne Boleyn**
*c.1501-1536*

*I have heard the executioner is very good,*
*and I have a little neck.*


In retrospect
excising the sizable mole
on her neck

or slicing off the extra
finger on her left hand

could not have saved her

In her grave
she lies
in an old arrow box

too short for her body
her head resting
beside her

no coffin provided

**Amelia Earhart**
*1897-1937?*


struck the word "obey"
from her wedding vows
wrote her own pre-nup

spelling out the terms of
her marriage to publisher Putnam

*I shall not hold you*
*to any medieval code*
*of faithfulness*

*nor shall I consider myself*
*bound to you*

*Please let us not interfere*
*with the other's work or play*

*I may have to keep someplace*
*where I can go to be myself*
*now and then*

*I cannot guarantee to endure*
*at all times the confinement*
*of even an attractive cage*

## The Hollywood Sign Girl
*1908 -1932*


Blonde starlet
without work
removes her black
and tan silk coat

folds it alongside
her stylish purse
a suicide note inside

climbs the ladder
at the base
of the letter "H"

throws herself over

Some say her ghost
still makes itself known

walking out of the fog
late at night

the pungent smell
of gardenias floating

## Jayne Mansfield
*1933 -1967*

Brainy brunette
Vera Jane Palmer

hawked books door to door
sold candy and popcorn

taught dance to pay for
acting classes

(Her prominent breasts
considered problematic

she lost her first job
modeling bathing suits

around a pool
for General Electric)

dropped her bikini top
at a press junket

to become Hollywood's
dumb blonde

spoke in a soft-voiced coo
punctuated with squeals

became less than real
Jayne Mansfield

**The Bonnie Parker Monologue**
*1910 -1934*


On that fateful May day
ambushed and betrayed

I lay vivid and dead
in my rusty red dress

words I wrote
in a long-ago notebook

*"Don't nothing ever happen
around here?"*

floating with the vultures
overhead and near

## Sylvia Plath Ruminating
*1932 -1963*


So warm
and comforting here
in the oven

the red balloon
in my head
imploding

**Anne Sexton Talking to Herself**
*1928 -1974*


*Frozen*
*no map*
*no road*

*a gray foggy wall*
*a stone that lives*

*I am a collection*
*of dismantled almosts*
*queen of all my sins*

*In my head*
*I'm undergoing*
*open heart surgery*

My words anoint me

**Flannery O'Connor**
*1925 -1964*


In love with birds
she purchased

by mail order
a pair of peacocks in 1952

The cackling crowd
at Andalusia grew loud

their squeals sounding in her words
"like a cheer from an invisible parade"

In letters she gave away
discarded tail feathers

said in her essay, "In the end
the last word will be theirs"

**Sister Rosetta Tharpe**
*1915 -1973*


Rediscovered in the 70s
a "blacked-up Elvis in drag"

self-taught prodigy
before the King

she honed her skills
on street corners
in the 40s

finger-picking
her electric guitar

strutting, hot-dogging
shredding and wind-milling

boundary-bending
bi-sexual black woman
from the South

"one foot in Saturday night
one in Sunday morning"

too secular for gospel
too sacred for soul

reborn godmother
of rock and roll

**Janis Joplin**
*1943 -1970*

A belt of
Southern Comfort
and a feather boa

transformed
a tortured, vulnerable girl
from Port Arthur, Texas

into a pearl

**Little Miss Sure Shot**

*Annie Oakley*
*1860 -1926*


To survive
Phoebe Ann Moses

learned to shoot at eight
her father's rifle

married her first rival
Frank Butler

could split a playing
card edgewise

or snuff out the flame
of a burning candle

joined Buffalo Bill's
Wild West Show

became Annie Oakley
performed for Queen Victoria

shot the ashes off a cigarette
held by the German Kaiser

went to Paris
toured Europe

became a legend
in her own time

may have died
from lead exposure

**Inventory**

*Patsy Cline*
*1932 -1963*


*Items recovered:*
Cline's wristwatch
stopped at 6:25

Confederate flag
cigarette lighter

studded belt
gold lamé slippers

*Note:*
Attire and money from
last performance
never found

in the remote site
where the plane
went down

## Portraiture in Stardust

*Susanna Clark*
*1939 -2012*


Lonestar tunesmith Guy Clark
remembers Susanna his wife
writing songs on a dare

swears hers rode higher
on the charts
than his own

An artist she painted
his iconic first cover
and Willie's *Stardust*

Clark calls her his queen
confesses he treated her
less than one

recalls a time
he and Townes
were in the house day-drunk

when someone snapped
a picture of Susanna
who had had enough

Because of his carousing
Susanna left Guy for four years
but always kept in touch

finally calling him up
saying she couldn't live alone
and was coming home

Guy thinks Townes
was her true soul mate

(though Shel Silverstein
often dropped by
"after Susanna," says Guy)


She went into a long slide
when Townes died
never recovering

For years she stayed in bed
in her gown
Guy bearing the brunt

She died one night around midnight
after Guy slipped in bed beside her
a long bout of songwriting

behind him

**To Zelda**
*1900-1948*

*Zelda Fitzgerald, identified only by her slipper,*
*died in a fire at Highlands Hospital*
*in Asheville, NC, March 10, 1948*


Zelda
In your dancing shoes

why couldn't you choose
your way to die
in the sweet summer's sunset

why couldn't you
let the end come
and pluck it like a choice plum

from the off-limits tree
that grew in the shining pool
with roots in the sky?

# Love And Marriage

### The Dancers

Awakened by her breath
against his chest he touches
the cool perfect roundness
of one shoulder which shone
last night like a smooth white stone
and traces with his forefinger
the bone that leads to the soft sunken place
at the base of her throat
feels the warmth of her breast
then lets his hand rest

## Son of Somnus

The moon cuts in
like an insult
its watery rays leading to your face

You lie in the light
insubstantial as a dream

Awakened, shaken by the view
I lie on my side
watching you

I feel you slipping away

As the night's cover
strains over the breaking day
I rise to push it away

I yearn to see you
bearded and imperfect
not journeying with the night's
metaphysical miles

You stir. I turn
still cold and alone
to receive your sleepy smile

**Pretty-by-Night**


Last night
(was it a dream?)
I bloomed into a dark-haired
lady of the night

The room
pale blue island shimmered
I lay in soft shifting water
lulled by whispered leaf voices

Today I awaken
in a silent room
closed as a tomb
neutral as wood

doomed by daylight

**Dreamer**

Golden lids lit
like translucent moons

Odysseus-like
you are caught in the clutches
of rosy-fingered dawn

Networks of red and blue veins
course through your closed orbs
tracing your epic napping

As your eyelids twitch
and lift like the shades
of night

I wish that I might be
patient Penelope
guiding your journey homeward

## Dreamscape

Swimming in silver
I rise
my life
a skin I have shed

Eyes glittering
graceful as a snake
I stir my starry skies
and breathe like Eve

onto my lover's bed

## Discovery

*People search for love as if it were a city lost . . .*
Diane Ackerman

What is it
about you
that haunts me
so much?

I want
to discover
your heart

to feel it
lying there
bare, apart

hot to the touch

**In the Dark**

*Like a fire in a dry thicket...*
Louise Bogan


In the dark
in his arms
where the sunburn
and freckles
don't show

she flows
over him
like sweet honeysuckle

He tastes
her nectar

## Proposal

At the sound
of her

he unspooled
from the barstool

moved through
the crowded room

wound himself
around her

smooth-danced her
to his music

until he had
his answer

**Marriage**

Fifteen
and not many chances
for courting

When they say
her husband
picked her
like a flower
from his first wife's grave
(new mother for
his four children)
it is so

A quick stab of pain
a drop of blood
she made her peace
with passion

It is hardscrabble life
she romances now

# Signs

*When you go looking for what's lost, everything is a sign.*
Eudora Welty

I have not bled
this month, Mother
and I am afraid

Just yesterday
a bird flew into the living room
losing its way

I didn't sleep a wink last night
A dog howled outside my window
and the clock didn't strike

Must have been midnight
I saw Will's first wife plain as day
standing over my bed

glistening with sweat
crying with no sound
holding her dead baby

all the while
Will still sleeping
beside me

I felt the same fear
I saw in her face
this time last year

You remember, don't you Mother?
You asked me to help with the birthing
It was my first time

You cut cotton strips
and bound her wrists
to the bedposts

I placed the small, round stick
you handed me
in her mouth

bathed her face
as you commanded her
to bear down

I remember most the silence
as I watched you wrap the baby—stillborn
in the same soft cloth

And I can never forget the look
in Will's eyes at the funeral
when he finally raised them

and gazed at me
as if seeing me
for the first time

Tiny shivers
ran up and down my spine
and my whole body shook

as he took a sprig of white lilac
from his wife's casket
and handed it to me

Will's out there now
on the front porch
drinking his coffee

staring over the valley
looking at rows and rows
of newly-planted fields

seeing the cattle
grazing on the hill
below the graveyard

the headstone visible still
in its rising up
and shining in the light

**Shivaree**

Having jumped the broom
in her Sunday-go-to-meeting clothes
and her only pair of shoes
she steps close to the affray
over the threshold
out of the frying pan
into the fire

# The Speed of Grace

*Thou didst put me together in my mother's womb.*
*I am fearfully and wonderfully made . . .*
                    Psalm 139

Nine days weary and worn
choleric and childbirth-ridden
graceless and ashamed

she has lain
against the counterpane
watching her husband

hovering above her
braiding and
re-braiding her hair

It is an image she cannot bear

Fever raging she rises
finds her husband's straight-edged razor
lifts its ivory handle to her head

Shed of frame and shorn
blood like tears in her eyes
salty and warm

she is begirded and reborn

# Traces

Voracious as hounds
snowflakes thickening
before their eyes
they run the traces
tracking trees
searching for evergreen

When they reach the top
their breath cutting like knives
he fells the perfect one
his hatchet hacking the silence
making quick, raspy sounds
not unlike gasps

Spent, their lips licking flakes
saltiness on their tongues
they sink weightless
into the white
melting like flames
felled by love

# Love Hurts

**Body x Two**


Body x two
and I am you

Sinew and bone
I atone

Paint-enhanced
subdued

imbued with lewd
intellect eschewed

my womb
entombs

while your balls
balance you

## Temptation

There's nothing
more appealing
than early-ripening fruit

fresh, firm flesh
slightly sweet
ready to eat

## Betrayal

In a letter he wrote
in a beautiful hand
he begged her forgiveness

for the stone
he had laid on her heart

the burden he had placed
on her shoulders

but told her
she bore most of the blame

her eyes shiny and haunting
her cheeks aflame

her body white and glowing
as the inside
of a porcelain bowl

## Fragile Freeways

Life
was laid out
so neatly

leading
straight
home

until
you drove
by

and the road
became a dark question mark
serpentine under a lonely sky

## Traveling Music

You sit on your side of the car
marking your territory
one arm thrown carelessly out the window
resting on the rolled-down glass
the other barely touching the steering wheel
moving it magically

I admire your profile
tough, brown, and handsome
but I wouldn't want to say so
I've learned that about you
You'd rather things were left unsaid
and sometimes consider talking a slight

I suppose I like that about you
One doesn't have to shout
Still, given half the chance
I'd like to see your eyes
linger rather than glance

A little traveling music, you say
I flip on the radio
and forward we fly
into the darkness together
as the night settles

## Woman on the Porch

*. . . sinking in black water . . .*
   Joyce Carol Oates


Young-old face
with aged eyes
watches the traffic race
up and down the road

A trace of music floats
from an open convertible
teenagers' hair blowing

The woman on the porch
swats away a fly
crosses her legs
can't feel a thing

keeping time
like a metronome
to some lost song
in her head

played long ago
on another car radio
taking her so far back

into the black void
she can no longer
hear the birds sing

# Idaho

Uncle Jeff
dropping everything
ran off to Idaho
with Aunt Ida
stayed all
of one week
before he came crawling
back home
with his tail tucked
between his legs
like a sheep-killing dog
Aunt Pallie standing
in the front door
waiting for him
a soft, umber statue
in the dark
holding a cup
in her hands

*come back, baby*
*come on home*
*supper's ready*
*bread's done*
*your coffee's hot*

**Lighting the Fire**

*. . . nothing to burn but paper . . .*
    Hilda Morley

Field flowers
once crushed by young bodies
in the act of lovemaking

have many times sprung up
furling themselves
towards the sun

She walks the dusty road
remembers the charm
of an arm on her back
fingers tracing a map on her face
lips touching the nape of her neck

But the hard spur of living chafes
chars her emotions
strips bare her soul
exposes old scars
leaves her cold

Alone in her cabin
she folds her memories
in the lockbox of her brain

strikes a match
lights the fire
watches it burn

## Old Age Penchant

He paces by the door
waiting for the mailman
impatient for his monthly "draw"

She sits by the fire
baking her legs
until raw

The next day he goes to the store
buys nylons and step-ins with lace
soft as a young girl's face

His wife
finds them
in his hiding place

*Yours*, he lies
offering them up
as sacrifice

the gulf between them
too deep, too treacherous
too wide to cross

## Je Regrette

Lying in a bed
still scarred by the shape
of her lover's body

she conjures
a sharpened and marred
version of him

ensconced
in another
woman's arms

Rising from her warm grave
she erases his face
discards all traces of him

embarks on a dark
and lonely odyssey
homeward

## End Game

Together they stay
intertwined like winding sheets
seeking succor
sucking substance
growing into one another
like parasites
failing to see
the darkness coming

# Our House

**Epos**

*Once you dip your toe in Big Ivy
you never want to leave.*
        —Legend


Absalom
eloped with his 15-year-old sweetheart
swam the Swannanoa
with his bride-to-be on his back
bought the first Big Ivy tract

built a home
in the mountain valley
out of hand-hewn logs
a chimney of native stone
and a hearthstone of flint

planted an apple orchard
a grape arbor
and a garden
part vegetable
part old-fashioned flower

and stinging nettles
around his natural spring

It stood for one hundred years
its razing marked the end of an era

Big Ivy
named for mountain laurel
or ivy that grew
along its banks

Big Ivy
Big Creek
Haw Branch
Sugar Creek


There is a landscape
of the heart
that sets us apart
the spill and dark sparkle
of water
that runs deep
cuts to the core
through six generations and more

There is a landscape
of the heart
that sets us apart

the Corner Rock
the Snake Den
the Coleman Boundary

the Pinnacle
Balsam Gap
Mount Mitchell
Craggy

**Legacy**


My aunt sat on her front porch
in a chair bottomed with strips of tires
swinging her crossed leg, dipping snuff

*Your great-grandmother ruled*
*with an iron hand*
*and Grandpa was a rounder*

*owned land as far as the eye can see*
*all the way up to the Coleman Boundary*

*They say he courted her by bringing armfuls of flowers*
*picked by the roadside or out of other people's yards*
*traded his mule for a chestnut mare*

*carried her around in a hand basket after they were married*
*all the while making time with the hired help*

A smile threatened the corners of my aunt's wrinkled mouth
and a small rivulet of snuff ran down one side

*After he died*
*Grandma didn't take to widow's weeds*
*said they didn't become her*

*She'd sit on the porch cooling Sunday afternoons in the summer*
*after cooking cut-off corn and baking soft butter biscuits*
*She'd throw back her head and cackle*

*I ought to have taken me a young lover*
*just to bedevil Elbert, she'd say*

*but he'd have dragged chains up and down the stairs at night*
*and, after my laying out, danced on my grave for spite*

My aunt's face softened
A long time passed before she spoke again

*We grandchildren would play on the porch*
*run the length of it back and forth*
*like fighting fire*

*or stand under the arbor eating pink grapes*
*clear as glass and sweet as honey*
*bees buzzing a halo over our heads*

*Sometimes when I look really hard*
*I can just see Grandma*
*coming over the ridge*

*her bright apron glowing*
*waving like a flag*
*calling me home*

**Americana Rural**

I
*c. 1930*

Her daddy stands bespectacled
in his photograph
beside a piteous Standard Oil pump
Vulcan hardware, Hillside plows
and an incongruous bubble gum machine

ragged coat
heavy, rolled trousers
worn canvas shoes
yet proud in his dandy vest and watch fob
white shirt and tie

perhaps seeing beyond
the clutter and rubble
of his little country store
set in the red clay like stone

beyond the backbreaking debt
of unpaid loans and extended credit
of desperate neighbors

And all she remembers now
is the day she stole from him

Ready to close for the day
he laid his stained apron

on the counter
went to crank the old Model T

*It was like poetry*
*watching the shiny pieces of candy*
*multicolored as marbles*
*fall into the upright umbrella*

As she stumbled
into the car beside him
the ungainly umbrella tumbled over
spilling a stream of cellophane
on the seat and floorboard
He turned and looked at her—
still there, that twinkle in his eye
for a favorite if impulsive child—
and all he could say was
I don't mind you taking a piece or two
but next time don't take it all

His battered beret blurred
before her fall

## II
### c. 1940

*It was like poetry*
*the way he moved*
*his finely formed hand*
*that Sunday morning*
*smoking in the front seat*
*of the car*

*first to his mouth*
*then dangling it elegantly*
*out the open window*
*carelessly flicking away the ashes*
*from his cigarette*

*his hand floating in the wind*
*delicate as a dancer's*

He drove the borrowed car
over the state line
She was seventeen
he, twenty-five

They eloped
to South Carolina shore
sand running
in the warm April sun
shining like the diamond
she would never have
her future spreading out before her
like an umbrella opening

## 1950: Rearview

*She forearms the flower from sight and fogs the view again.*
    Sarah Kennedy

We trace our names
in the car window's dusty glass
pile into the back seat

elbowing each other
reading signs as we travel
over narrow, winding roads

At the hospital Mother eases
into the front seat
cradling the baby

a tuft of black fuzz visible
above a wizened red face

She admonishes us not to touch
the soft, sunken place
on the top of the head

as we breathe in one motion
the din of our voices
hushed by the holy moment

**Moving On**


We sat in the back seat
of the black humpback car
parked behind the smokehouse
smelling of cigarettes and aftershave

We drank Kool-Aid
ate bologna sandwiches
on Bunny bread
traveled to imaginary places

Sun spilling in our laps
lulling us to half-sleep
we imagined Daddy
tuning the radio

Sunday mornings on the way to church
we heard the squishing
and twisting of sound
until he found WWNC

The Chuck Wagon Gang sang
"Precious Memories" in close harmony
their words tumbling out of the dashboard
Daddy humming or singing along

Saturday nights he'd tune to WSM
listen to the Grand Ole Opry
drive us to the store
for Push-Ups and Nehi's

Let's Hank Snow, he said
when we'd get back home
meaning time for bed
Then we'd go to sleep
the nasal sounds of
*I'm moving on, I'll soon be gone*
echoing in our heads

## The Root of It All

*. . . whatever you have to say, leave
the roots on . . .*
        Charles Olson


Mid tangle of honeysuckle
a baby bird, dun-colored
mouth open, soundless
still as a rock, huddles

My sisters and I
take turns cradling the bird
fragile as an egg
ticking like a time-bomb

Stumps, severed heads, frown
Mosquitoes draw blood
Broom sedge cuts

A tree's arm
wipes out the sun
Steel-winged snake feeders
circle, hover

A copper-colored
narrow fellow
glides into brackish water
gives us the evil eye

Through the dusk
Mother's voice
echoes ghostly

We rest the baby bird
in its nearby nest
camouflaged
hard to find

Then home to roots
and roost
we fly

**Blackberries**

*Big as the ball of my thumb, and dumb as eyes*
Sylvia Plath


The day dew bloomed
in Mother's eye
she rose before sunrise
to pick blackberries

Five years old
that summer before he died
I sat on Grandpa's lap
at the end of the porch
to catch first light

while she went
up the hill
above the house
to fill her pails
before the dew dried
or anyone else arrived

We ate the jam
savored the pies
drank the juice
for stomach aches
while Mother felt
the infection rise

Forever after
she had a blind spot
black as a berry, she said
in her right eye

## Decorum

When Mother
sent us
down the road
around the bank
or up the lane

to borrow a cup
of meal or flour
she taught us to say
we'll pay you back
when Daddy gets paid

and cautioned us
never to open up
anyone's refrigerator
or touch a thing

and to say no thank you
if they asked us
to stay for supper

## Distances

We woke to the sight
of a coon lying
on the cold hearth

so still and perfect
dead eyes staring

Hardly breathing
we edged out of the bed
and encircled it

Daddy's face floating
from the distance
of an open door

the worn wooden floor
like an ocean
between us

## Jole Blon

Daddy called me "Jody Blond"
a corruption of
the popular old Cajun tune

cut my hair
with a pair of scissors
used to cut horses' manes

curled my sister's hair
with strips of brown paper

silences piling up
like shorn locks

on the floor
of the high front porch

## Animal Attraction

Daddy spread a tow sack
on the horse's back

cupped his hands
made a stirrup

I put my foot in it
and he hoisted me up

I grabbed onto the mane
held on tight

nothing but horseflesh
rough against bare legs

pungent smell of sweat
the rhythm of muscles

soft plunk of hooves
as Daddy led us up

to the pasture gate
the sun shining

like a torch
in the dusk

## Gnat Smoke

When they swarmed
in great waves
on warm summer nights

we stuffed damp rags
and a handful of shavings
into tin cans and lit them

sat with family and neighbors
in the chip yard
until drowsy

then found our way
to the house
where we washed bare feet

dirty hands and faces
in the kitchen sink
before stumbling to bed

the music of jar flies
and laughter drifting
through open windows

seeping like smoke
into sleep
and dreams

## Summer Etude

Tommy toes multiply
split open in their ripeness

Crook-necked squash
curl like tiny kittens

Cucumbers hide
in viny darkness

Zinnias and marigolds
glow by the paling

Lithe, lean bodies
always in motion
reach for the sky

Frogs holler at dusk
and lightning bugs

set the world on fire

# God Bless The Child

**Childhood**

I
am
a
husk

Cut
thin
my
skin

so
everyone
can
see
in

## In the Pasture

a child's toe
nudges
a weathered skull's face

cradling Queen Anne's Lace
murmuring *murder*
*body never found*

Overhead
vultures circle
round

**Park Swing**

Little girls
with horizontal hair
and umbrella dresses
punch holes in the sky

## Southern Night Pattern: Storm Rising

A young girl
in a faded print dress
sits in a chip yard
in the unnatural calm

listening
to the dull
thud of ax
on wood

I'll Fly Away

*When I die, Hallelujah, by and by, I'll fly away . . .*


My mother carried me for eleven and a half months
or so she said, but people said, Laci
just lost her notching stick
that's all there is to it
Well, anyway, I was born
I took a long time to get here
but somehow I felt I was always
just on the verge of leaving, you know?
Take the time I went with my sisters
to our cousin's pond
Mother told us not to go
She always was deathly afraid of water
she told us later
I lost my balance as I was looking
into the water and fell in and went all the way
under—I drowned, I think, because I saw stars
and sky that wouldn't stop and I heard music
celestial-like, or so I thought
Or take the time I was on my way up Grandma's
lane and got caught in a summer downpour—
a real toad-stringer—raindrops as big as silver dollars
The sky turned dark and hail fell
big as baseballs
and Grandma said, Little Birdie
you're not bigger than a minute—
the wind's going to pick you up one day
and blow you away! I felt like it might, too

and I'd just fly away home like a bird
Or take the time in spring
when I lay down in the new grassy yard
and the clouds took me on a ride
and I shut my eyes and went to Heaven
then and there—I don't know
where the time went, do you?—
and I couldn't feel a thing
But I think the time I really wanted to go—
I mean really fly away—was the day
our neighbor took me to his apple house
to give our family some Sheepnoses
he'd kept over the winter and the smell
of old cold caught in my throat
when he lifted the latch
and closed the door behind us
and his great blank shadow touched me—
I just put me on a pair of silver wings
and flew right out of there, you know?

## Whiskey Ballet

The other man
bandy-legged
shorter than my father
who stood ramrod straight—

two silhouettes
breathing like engines
in the cold November night

dancing in the dark
distilling spirits
filling jars

while unobserved
a distance away
a child starts
swayed with pain

heart-scarred
forever changed
spilling secrets
to the stars

## Knowing

The young girl
came in the door
to a cold house

saw the bed frame
stripped to the thin
mattress and springs

where her mother's blood
had bled a flower
clean through to the floor

and could only guess
at the power of the word
*miscarriage*

when she saw
the terror and pain
on her father's face

as he commanded her
to get the wash pan
and clean up the mess

# If I Had A Bell

**In the Garden**

*fall*, from the Old English *feallan*, to fall down


Under molten skies
she spies
Henry
black-as-indigo
field hand

spread out
like a week's washing
against the fence stobs
head back
arms akimbo

She opens
her mouth
ready to go
into her familiar
rigamarole

Henry, you been out all night—
got tight—didn't make it home?

when
she sees
he's still
as some old
scarecrow

while a bird
pecks at
one of his eyes
as if his face were
a discarded corncob

**Emmett Lewis "Bobo" Till**
*1941-1955*


They killed you
because you were
a 14-year-old boy who
whistled at a white woman
at a grocery store
in Money, Mississippi

A teen out of Chicago
you didn't understand
you had broken
an unwritten Jim Crow law
of the South

Four days later
two white men
dragged you out
of your bed
in the dead
of the night

beat you
gouged out
your right eye
shot you
with a .45 caliber pistol
then tied a 75-pound
cotton gin fan
around your neck

with barbed wire
to weigh you down
and dropped your body
into the Tallahatchie

where it was found
three days later
identifiable only
by the ring
you were wearing



Your killers
acquitted
by an all-male
white jury
who took
a "soda break"
to stretch
deliberations
to one hour

then sold their story
to *Look* magazine
for money

## Conviction

Through the yard
the bloodhounds ran
tracking a loose convict

It happened in the hen house
When she lifted the latch
the convict rose before her
like Lazarus

One breast in his hand
he tore at her clothes
then disappeared
like an apparition
into the woods

She rose on watery legs
gathered her eggs
into her worn felt hat
without breaking one

She heard it coming
from a long way off
a persistent buzzing
in her head
like the droning of bees

It was her own voice
spiraling within her
dark and coiled

writing like a snake
ready to strike

her scream
raping the morning's silence

## Colloquy in Black and White

The churches are quiet and cool
that August day in 1962
Men in suits
and women in shirtwaists, white gloves, and shoes
line the pews

From pulpits, black-robed preachers
praise us upon our graduation
from high school
speak of conversion
and send us forth
with the King James Version
of the New Testament
in cadenced form

*Though I speak with the tongues of angels*
*and have not love*
*I have become as sounding brass*
*or tinkling cymbal*

Far away in a town
known as Hollywood
the body of Marilyn Monroe
removed from her LA home
lies in a morgue
under a sheet
cold to the coroner's touch
according to reports

a "possible suicide"
from an overdose of Nebutal

John Houston
director on her last film
says after her death
"She fought her enemy
consciousness
with sedatives"

At college that fall
they awaken us
from sleep and dreams
rout us out at dawn
wearing only cold sheets
herd us like sheep
down to the gymnasium
for the annual "freshmen examination"

First they take us
one by one
into a cubicle
windowless and claustrophobic
lit by a bright strobe
where they force us to disrobe
and shoot us nude
twice from either side
and once "full frontal"

then onward we trod
around the room
like cattle or chattel

*Like Headlines - 96*

to the doctors' domain
where they peel back our sheets
for the universal "feel"

Numbed and shocked
we fight like Marilyn
our consciousness
and for survival
honor the invitation
slip on our little black dresses
and go for tea
with the college president

# The Marilyn Interview

1. Is it true you said, "Hollywood is a place where they'll pay you a thousand dollars for a kiss and fifty cents for your soul?"
2. Is it true that one of your earliest memories is being almost smothered by your mother with a pillow when you were two years old?
3. Is it true at the age of nine you were confined to an LA orphans' home where they paid you a nickel a month for kitchen work while taking back a penny every Sunday for church?
4. Is it true they raped you?
5. Is it true you had a lisp and stuttered?
6. Is it true you wrote poems, enjoyed literature, and regretted never finishing school?
7. Is it true, at sixteen, you married a man in the Merchant Marines you called "Daddy"?
8. Is it true you were born blonde but went "mousy"?
9. Is it true during World War II you worked in an airline factory spraying parts with flame retardant?
10. Is it true they called you the "Blonde Bombshell"?
11. Is it true "Joltin' Joe" DiMaggio beat you?
12. Is it true you owned over 200 books including Milton, Whitman, and Tolstoy, and that you listened to Beethoven?
13. Is it true you were once voted "Miss Artichoke"?
14. Is it true the famous birthmark above your lip wasn't fake but real—a very pale mole you darkened with makeup?
15. Is it true you shaved a quarter of an inch off the heels of your shoes to accent the wiggle in your walk?
16. Is it true a studio once suspended you for not reporting to work on *The Girl in Pink Tights* and *How to Be Very, Very Popular*?
17. Is it true that you won a Golden Globe for your role as constantly

drinking loose chanteuse Sugar Cane in *Some Like It Hot* and another nomination for café singer Cherie in *Bus Stop*?

18. Is it true Billy Wilder said you had breasts "like concrete" and a brain like "Swiss cheese"?

19. Is it true you were *Playboy* magazine's first nude centerfold and "Sweetheart of the Month" in '53?

20. Is it true Marilyn Manson took his first name in homage to you?

21. Is it true that in Norway there is a life-size statue of you?

22. Is it true you said you'd trade all your fame for "one little baby"?

23. Is it true Sinatra gave you a Maltese puppy you named "Maf Honey"?

24. Is it true Arthur Miller called you "a poet on the street trying to recite to a crowd pulling at your clothes"?

25. Is it true you paid his wife alimony?

26. Is it true that the jewels you wore when you sang "Diamonds Are a Girl's Best Friend" were really rhinestones?

27. Is it true you had a one-night stand with Joan Crawford and when you refused to repeat it she became "spiteful"?

28. Is it true you said, "It's all make-believe, isn't it"?

29. Is it true they admitted you to the Payne Whitney Psychiatric Clinic and placed you on the ward for the most seriously disturbed?

30. Is it true they credited you with the first nude scene in a major film *Something's Got to Give* and then they fired you for drug dependency and chronic lateness?

31. Is it true your face graces the first stamp in USPS's "Legends of Hollywood" series?

32. Is it true *People* magazine voted you "Sexiest Woman of the Century" in 1999?

33. Is it true you said, "You can't be sexy all the time?"

34. Is it true you also said, "It's better for the world to have known you as a sex symbol than never to have known you at all?"

35. Is it true they found you nude in bed alone in your home dead with a phone in your hand?
36. Is it true they murdered you?

# Beauty

Rilke got it right—
beauty is nothing but terror

wear it like a crown
it will take you down

Monroe and Stratton tried it
died for their trouble

Can't trust it

neck thrust our
marred with peacock envy

dark blue as if a serpent
had kissed it

Lucifer before the fall

# A Caution

*Every heart is dark half the time.*
            Josh Ritter


At a certain age
she stops meeting

the eyes of young men
on the street

admiring their virile bodies
their easy gaits, their grace

stops gazing
at her face

annihilates
her smile

chucks the tease
in her voice

holds a funeral
for her youth

a wake
for her fate

bleeds out
on a page

of *Vanity Fair*
magazine

**Nine Lives**

*I am a smiling woman . . .*
*And like the cat I have nine times to die.*
      Sylvia Plath


1.  She said, "Attention must be paid."
    He said, "Let's get laid."

2.  She said, "Help me to know the opposite sex."
    He said, "Let's have sex."

3.  She said, "I am strong and independent."
    He said, "I'll make you weak and dependent."

4.  She said, "All of life is precious."
    He said, "Assume the position, bitch."

5.  She said, "I see the good in mankind."
    He said, "You have no eyes. Try more makeup."

6.  She said, "Let's be friends."
    He said, "Sexual harassment will not be reported here but will be graded."

7.  She said, "You have the power to do good."
    He said, "I have the power."

8.  She said, "You have a nice smile."
    He said, "You have a nice behind."

9. She said, "Please help me. "I want to try . . . "
   He said, "I'll bleed you dry."

**Abortion State**


In the Fifties, she was our next-door neighbor
When Ike beat Adlai we watched the returns on her TV
She gave my mother a home perm and made
little checkered shirts for my older sister and me

One Sunday morning I rode to church with her
in her neat, white Chevrolet
She wore a sleeveless dress with a full, swinging skirt
her hair upswept, tinted black and lacquered
She wore perfume and makeup
I sat in the front seat
She smiled at me and treated me like a grownup
Once she let me choose two pair of earrings
from her jewelry chest to play with—then let me keep them

One summer day she inserted a coat hanger into herself
almost bled to death on her neatly pressed white sheets

Weeks later, as she cut with a long, sharp knife
precise slices of cake she had made
and decorated for her son's birthday
I looked for a sign—blood on her hands—
but there was none
She smiled at me as she scooped homemade
peach ice cream on my plate
She looked the same—but she wasn't

Afterwards, when I complained
of a stomach ache and sat on the porch

in the white, enameled swing
and wouldn't play games anymore
like "kick the can" and "hide and seek"
I felt a sadness come over me
that even I could not explain

## Late Autumn: A Valediction

The bungalow next door
lit by maple trees
housed a family of four
seemed serene

before the morning
head shorn and forlorn
the wife immolated herself
with an acetylene torch

became a flame
red as the lone leaf
that settled itself against
the scorched front porch

## Outside the Lines

*Matthew Shepard*
*1976 -1998*

*. . . love's like smoke beyond all repair.*
                Leonard Cohen


Young blond boy
nailed, impaled
on a fence

crucified for straying
outside the lines

## Quarry

—from the Latin *cor*, "heart"


They all told us how the neighbor's son
had escaped the mental hospital
and was on the run

how the posse found him
quarry in the dark
hunkered under a rock

on the mountaintop
hungry and cold
feet bleeding in the snow

how the law officers
had drawn their guns
but had not fired a shot

## Daddy's Girl

With a wink and a leer
her daddy holds
the cold open can of beer
tantalizingly near

tickling her nose
Through bow-like lips
eager as a baby bird
she sates her thirst

with a single sip
laughs a giggly
hiccupping laugh
then burps

Putting up one perfect hand
she catches a trickle of froth
as it bursts like broth
from her soft pink mouth

## Porcelain

They all said
she was the prettiest girl
they had ever seen

blue eyes
black curls
porcelain skin

rosebud mouth
floating face down
wanting to speak

**Road/Kill**

I

You lie
on the highway

delicate spine
non-aligned

fawn-soft fur bathed
in red glaze

II

I die
in my driveway

askew and nude
legs splayed

face erased
mouth agape

still
calling his name

# Pet Sounds

### Cat's Eye

hypnotizes
tail a metronome

Cat travels light
brings whole other
worlds in tow

spirit disappearing
mid beehives of people
trolls under the bridge
roosters crowing at dusk
bloody sunsets

reborn in a barn
exploring the chimera
of old boards
honeysuckle vine
jar fly's drone

prowling through woods
reading leaves like palms
finding fortunes in slippery rocks
bogs, sudden storms
wind blurring vision
eyes watering

I find it true
to wrap myself

around the roughness
of ancient trees' skins
store light in my eyes
to see again

# Memory

One day my cat brought to me
what she thought was a gift
deposited on the porch for praise
a baby rabbit still breathing but barely

Panicked, I grabbed an empty flower bucket
scooped up the panting mass of brown fur
hurried through the grass at the yard's edge
placed it back in its mother's nest

carried my cat back to the garage
to her own bed
set the lock

Funny when I let her out the next day
how she forgot her hunger
ignored her water bowl
instead ran to the place
where she had dropped the body

sniffing and circling
bloodthirsty
haunting the spot
until dark

# Territories

The cat
curls around my feet

marking
its territory

completing
its circuitous journey

its liquid steps
blocking my path

sending me stumbling
fumbling towards love

softness in my arms
electric fur purring

## Snowfall

Like a fat, white cat dozing
the snow lingers
on doorsteps

Close as death
it snuggles
reining in the silence

smothering every sound
in the soft, white core
of its heart

**Omen**

*Patient till Paradise*
    Emily Dickinson


How easy
her limbs lie
in the snare of night

dreaming
the snow-white cat's
litheness

charming
the bed of rattlers
in the rock pile
in the garden
at the edge of Eden

## Symmetry

I woke at four
to the thunder of rain
pounding like pellets
against the windowpane

heard the wind
swooshing trees into
an incessant conversation

This morning I found

shiny leaves plastered
on spangled glass
saw outside
an immaculate white cat

wiped clean by its tiny
leaf-shaped tongue
sitting like a statue
in the sun

## Sleeper

Stars magnify themselves
the moon doubles

The furnace hums
sets loose the house
to circle the universe

An old ghost
traverses the rooms

comes to rest over the sleeper's breast
drops its hot breath on her cheek

with one electric finger enters her body
and opens the door to the past

*a pristine cabin*
*lush fields*
*wild life rioting*
*meadows exploding with color*
*clear water running*
*bees humming*

*chickens clucking*
*gardens thriving*
*greenness burning*
*and the coming of a perfect summer*

The sleeper nudges
the watching dog
listening on the porch
guarding the earth's harmony

before floating homeward
just as the furnace shuts off
sifting the silence until morning

# Epitaph

When it rained our little feist
frenzied by lightning and thunder
pushed himself inside

played hide-and-seek
under the kitchen table

*He would live forever it seemed*

posed for pictures
by the pump
even ate candy

went to the pasture
for butterflies
trailed us to the mail

went undercover in a kerchief
when my younger sister

kidnapped him for a day
to play in the barn

A bout with a snake bite
failed to take him out

Years later he went quietly
into the fields and died

We respected his wishes
for no funeral or eulogy

# When The Deal Goes Down

## Clearing the Cutter

I am clearing the clutter
a real dust up
that both elevates and deflates

Just when was I size 8
and am I still in love
with graffiti, mufti, and ink?

For the life of me
I don't know why
I feel so luckless

as I come and go in my intent
measuring out my life
in cardboard boxes and lint

Am I not glad to be free
raising windows, throwing caution
and curtains to the wind?

Maybe I'll settle then
erase traces
of all paltry rebellions

adjust to my robe and scuffs
and just one comfy chair
jettisoning my load

like the lone lush peony
in the glass bowl
on the table in the hall

soft pink petals
plummeting

**Mortality**


A clumsy terrapin
stumbles through high grass

tumbles past the garden gate
the old shed

disappears into
kudzu

tangled
honeysuckle

becomes
a piece

of dry wood
or gray rock

gut-startles
any time

it darkens
our path

## Obituary

I watched you
die today

There was no noise
and nothing slightly personal

They just
wheeled you
out

looking rather doubtful
about
resurrection

## Funeral

The sun was so hot
even the plastic flowers looked wilted

*"Isn't it a lovely day for a funeral?"*

The angry fist in my chest
beat against my best Sunday dress

*"I love the view from here."*


Aunt Pallie is dead, Daddy said
We went to pay our respects

I remember Uncle Jeff in a rocker
his features stone, light catching on his bald head

his bony hands moldy onion skin
with large, blue-black veins

*"He won't live long without her."*

I sat on the bed near the casket
and wondered where Aunt Pallie's legs were

# Elegy

When he was tight
he loved to play
sweet music
on the piano
stomping his feet
hunching over the keys
concentrating almost violently
on the rhythm
head bobbing
sweat beginning
over words fumbled for

Then late
with the other misfits
who walked the roads with him
and fell drunk indiscriminately
he found a church

He moaned
old-timey hymns
and Hank Williams
his cronies
shivering around
his radiant wet face

He was just beyond thirty
when they raided the place
and put him out of business

## Loss

Her hands small, strong
wanting to be busy

clasp the swing's chain
the place in her heart
an island of loss

I imagine
how she must have held

her lover's head
in those hands

with what energy
she entered into passion

Now she stills them
drops them to her side

in restive resignation
turns to me

takes the proffered pear
up to her mouth

bites it until the juices run

## Requiem

The land is silent and still
The pale sandy earth begs rain
Tobacco stands in long, even rows
leaves wilted like silken, green handkerchiefs

He walks with his familiar gait
legs slightly apart
hands crossed hard behind him
staring intently at the ground

He no longer wears his strange apparel
his funeral garments
His gray work shirt is darkened
by wings of sweat

The legs of his blue gallused overalls
rub against themselves

An errand, he says
We walk around the road
bruised with the beauty of bubbies

On the porch her summer cactus still blooms
her favorite color
She always wanted to be buried in red

She lingers in the room
in her Spring Flowers perfume
He fumbles among the stack of bills
stuck between the radio and the Bible

Answers to the federal government he dictates
as I write:
His wife has died

I close the door behind me
The oncoming roar of the usual afternoon shower
breaks the string in my mind

The calm is shot by the sweetest sound
as the first drops of rain begin to pound
the dry, thirsty ground

**Letter**

My dearest sister Serene

The church pews are almost empty
Every week there is at least one funeral
and the long walk up to the graveyard
gets harder and harder

The community is mute
the preacher too busy to sleep

The house frets with fever
When I am not on my knees
by my children's bed
I am emptying slop jars
or roasting onions for poultices

Winter seeps into our pores
Can't write anymore

Please pray for me

## After Influenza

She wanders
the graveyard
touches the stones
marking the graves
of the newly-dead
and remembers
one short season before
when all of them were alive

She sees the infant Banks boy
dark eyes glassy
from fever
tiny hands hot to the touch
his brave smile
as she applied the poultice
to his rattling chest

the little vein
in his forehead
beating wildly
then slowing
like a wound-down clock

# Burial

*. . . wood with a gift for burning*
              Adrienne Rich


Over the bridge
the wagon rattles, rumbles
carrying its onerous load
a plain wooden coffin

Under its weight
the frozen planks groan, sway
the team of horses
streaming in the cold
their manes undulating
alive in the light
their eyes blazing

## Tending the Graves

I see her coming with cuttings—
coleus, rose begonias
geraniums, impatiens

This spring day
she is making her yearly pilgrimage
to the graveyard on the hill

She will brush honeysuckle hair
from ancient faces
pluck star grass from their eyes

**Old Age**

*. . . the breath that never dies . . .*
*is the Mother of all creation . . .*
Lao Tzu


She sleeps deep
into the afternoon
having drawn the universe
back into herself

She sleeps
as I slept
in her womb

says she didn't sleep
her new world a possibility now
skin tender as a newborn

Nights I pass her room
in the dark
sighs too deep for words
breath that never dies

**Resolution**


Her resolve
is like looking
for lizards
in the creek

turning over
the rocks
waiting for the disturbance
to clear

**The Great Divide**

*The finest hour that I have ever seen*
*Is the one that comes in between.*
                    Kate Wolf


Like a shower
of flower petals
the tree sheds its yellow

The gray cat ducks
amid the flurry
scurries for shelter

pursued by birds
swooping down
to tackle

the only sound
through glass
as the wind passes

soft scratching
like mice
in the attic

Under cover
the harmonium
of faint breathing
the rising and falling

sighing and dying
on the air
like a prayer

**Resurrection**

*. . . I can see the light of a clear blue morning.*
                Dolly Parton


Wake to the velvet dawn
the softening darkness
of near morning

a bland overhead
of eggshell sky
not yet gone pastel

the lofty silence
lobbing dreams
your way

swaying between sleep
and awakening
nothing to hold you

to the night
just light coming
ever so gently to day

**Skydiving**

Free-falling
through life
is too easy

I'd rather float
with a discerning eye
earning my eternity

than to arrive
surprised
in paradise

# Progeny

I shall die
without a sound
in my grandmother's
late-summer garden

walking with her ghost
in the stun of the sun
under an October sky
shadows deepening and steepening

Stirred by the dull thud
of dug potatoes tumbling into a tin tub
and the whispering of dry leaves, wind-struck
I'll gather her words and sleep

And then in the spring I'll rise
like volunteer poppies—fragile, transparent, brilliant—
and sturdy larkspur strong as my daddy's back
and just as stubborn

I'll plant my poem
on hallowed ground

# Acknowledgments

Poems in this volume have appeared in the following venues:

"Maid of Orleans" in *Tender Curiosities*, Stone Ivy Press, 2016

"Anne Boleyn" in *Tender Curiosities*, Stone Ivy Press, 2016

"Amelia Earhart" in *Tender Curiosities*, Stone Ivy Press, 2016

"The Hollywood Sign Girl" in *Tender Curiosities*, Stone Ivy Press, 2016

"Jayne Mansfield" in *Tender Curiosities*, Stone Ivy Press, 2016

"The Bonnie Parker Monologue" in *Tender Curiosities*, Stone Ivy Press, 2016

"Sylvia Plath" in *Tender Curiosities*, Stone Ivy Press, 2016

"Anne Sexton Talking to Herself" in *Tender Curiosities*, Stone Ivy Press, 2016

"Flannery O'Connor" in *Tender Curiosities*, Stone Ivy Press, 2016

"Sister Rosetta Tharpe" in *Tender Curiosities*, Stone Ivy Press, 2016

"Janis Joplin" in *Tender Curiosities*, Stone Ivy Press, 2016

"Little Miss Sure Shot" in *Tender Curiosities*, Stone Ivy Press, 2016

"Inventory" in *Tender Curiosities*, Stone Ivy Press, 2016

"To Zelda" in *Tender Curiosities*, Stone Ivy Press, 2016

"The Dancers" in *New Ground*, WorldComm, 1998

"Son of Somnus" in *New Ground*, WorldComm, 1998

"Pretty-by-Night" in *The Ambiguity of Morning*, WorldComm, 2001

"Dreamer" in *The Ambiguity of Morning*, WorldComm, 2001

"Dreamscape" in *The Ambiguity of Morning*, WorldComm, 2001

"Discovery" in *The Ambiguity of Morning*, WorldComm, 2001

"In the Dark" in *First Light*, WorldComm, 2004

"Proposal" in *More Frailer than Flowers*, Aldrich Press, 2016

"Marriage" in *First Light*, WorldComm, 2004

"Signs" in *Colloquy in Black and White*, Catawba, 2009

"Shivaree" in *First Light*, WorldComm, 2004

"The Speed of Grace" in *The Ambiguity of Morning*, WorldComm, 2001

"Traces" in *The Ambiguity of Morning*, WorldComm, 2001

"Body x Two" in *New Ground*, WorldComm, 1998

"Temptation" in *First Light*, WorldComm, 1998

"Betrayal" in *More Frailer than Flowers*, Aldrich Press, 2016

"Fragile Freeways" in *The Arts Journal*

"Traveling Music" in *Americana Rural*, Wind Publications, 2012

"Woman on the Porch" in *1940: Poems*, Finishing Line Press, 2015

"Idaho" in *First Light*, WorldComm, 2004

"Lighting the Fire" in *1950: Poems*, Finishing Line Press, 2015

"Old Age Penchant" in *1950: Poems*, Finishing Line Press, 2015

"Je Regrette" in *More Frailer than Flowers*, Aldrich Press, 2016

"Epos" in *New Ground*, WorldComm, 1998

"Legacy" in *Colloquy in Black and White*, Catawba, 2009

"Americana Rural" in *Great Smokies Review*

"1950: Rearview" in *1950: Poems*, Finishing Line Press, 2015

"Moving On" in *Fresh*

"The Root of It All" in *1950: Poems*, Finishing Line Press, 2015

"Blackberries" in *1950: Poems*, Finishing Line Press, 2015

"Decorum" in *1950: Poems*, Finishing Line Press, 2015

"Jole Blon" in *1950: Poems*, Finishing Line Press, 2015

"Animal Attraction" in *1950: Poems*, Finishing Line Press, 2015

"Gnat Smoke" in *1950: Poems*, Finishing Line Press, 2015

"Summer Etude" in *1950: Poems*, Finishing Line Press, 2015

"Childhood" in *More Frailer than Flowers*, Aldrich Press, 2016

"In the Pasture" in *1950: Poems*, Finishing Line Press, 2015

"Park Swing" in *The Ambiguity of Morning*, WorldComm, 2001

"Southern Night Pattern: Storm Rising" in *The Ambiguity of Morning*, WorldComm 2001

"I'll Fly Away" in *The Ambiguity of Morning*, WorldComm, 2001

"Whiskey Ballet" in *The Ambiguity of Morning*, WorldComm, 2001

"Knowing" in *More Frailer than Flowers*, Aldrich Press, 2016

"In the Garden" *Asheville Poetry Review*

"Emmett Lewis 'Bobo' Till" in *Thanks for the Dark but That's Not Home*, Big Ivy Books, 2006

"Conviction" *in First Light*, WorldComm, 2004

"Colloquy in Black and White" in *Thanks for the Dark but That's Not Home*, Big Ivy Books, 2006

"The Marilyn Interview" in *Thanks for the Dark but That's Not Home*, Big Ivy Books, 2006

"Beauty" in *1950: Poems*, Finishing Line Press, 2015

"Nine Lives" in *Thanks for the Dark but That's Not Home*, Big Ivy Books, 2006

"Abortion State" in *Thanks for the Dark but That's Not Home*, Big Ivy Books, 2006

"Late Autumn: A Valediction" in *Horizons*, Stone Ivy Press, 2016

"Outside the Lines" in *1950: Poems*, Finishing Line Press, 2015

"Quarry" in *1950: Poems,* Finishing Line Press, 2015

"Daddy's Girl" in *Colloquy in Black and White*, Catawba, 2009

"Road/Kill" in *Colloquy in Black and White*, Catawba, 2009

"Cat's Eye" in *1950: Poems*, Finishing Line Press, 2015

"Memory" in *More Frailer than Flowers*, Aldrich Press, 2016

"Territories" in *The Ambiguity of Morning*, WorldComm, 2001

"Snowfall" in *The Ambiguity of Morning*, WorldComm, 2001

"Omen" in *First Light*, WorldComm, 2004

"Epitaph" in *More Frailer than Flowers*, Aldrich Press, 2016

"Clearing the Clutter" in *Colloquy in Black and White*, Catawba, 2009

"Obituary" in *New Ground*, WorldComm, 1998

"Funeral" in *New Ground*, WorldComm, 1998

"Elegy" in *New Ground*, WorldComm, 1998

"Requiem" in *New Ground*, WorldComm, 1998

"Letter" in *First Light*, WorldComm, 2004

"After Influenza" in *First Light*, WorldComm, 2004

"Burial" in *First Light*, WorldComm, 2004

"Tending the Graves" in *Home*, March Street Press, 2010

"Old Age" in *1950: Poems*, Finishing Line Press, 2015

"Resolution" in *First Light*, WorldComm, 2001

"The Great Divide" in *Horizons*, Stone Ivy Press, 2016

"Skydiving" in *New Ground*, WorldComm, 1998

"Progeny" in *Colloquy in Black and White*, Catawba, 2009

# About the Author

Nancy Dillingham's poetry, short fiction, and commentaries have appeared in various publications including *Asheville Poetry Review*, *Great Smokies Review*, Poetry in Plain Sight Project, *Rapid River Magazine*, *Fresh*, *The Lyricist*, *The Arts Journal*, *NC Literary Review*, *Bay Leaves*, *Half Tones to Jubilee*, *Pine Mountain Sand and Gravel*, *Old Mountain Press*, *Parting Gifts*, *Raleigh News & Observer*, *Asheville Citizen-Times*, *Mountain Xpress*, and *WNC Woman*.

She is the author of eleven books and chapbooks, a fictional memoir *Buried Lives: Memoir of a Survivor*, co-editor of four anthologies of western North Carolina women writers and collaborator on *Reflections in a River: Photographs by Joan Medlicott Haiku by Nancy Dillingham*. Her book of poems, *Home*, was nominated for a Southern Independent Book Award.

Nancy is a sixth-generation Dillingham from Big Ivy in western North Carolina. She lives in Asheville, NC.

www.ingramcontent.com/pod-product-compliance
Lightning Source LLC
LaVergne TN
LVHW011239080426
835509LV00005B/562